The ... to SPEED...NES

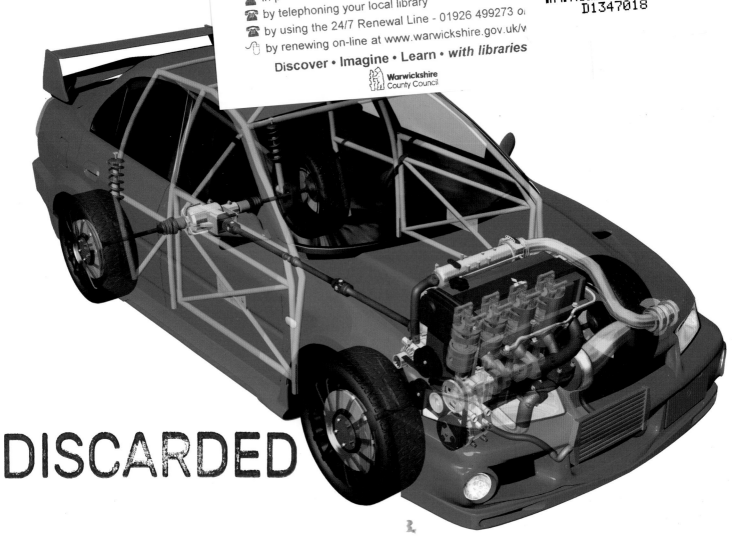

THE INSIDE AND OUT GUIDE TO SPEED MACHINES
was produced by

David West ⚇ Children's Books

7 Princeton Court
55 Felsham Road
London SW15 1AZ

Designer: Gary Jeffrey
Illustrators: Alex Pang and Moorhen Studios
Editor: Dominique Crowley
Consultant: William Moore
Picture Research: Victoria Cook

First published in Great Britain by Heinemann
Library, Halley Court, Jordan Hill, Oxford
OX2 8EJ, part of Harcourt Education.
Heinemann is a registered trademark
of Harcourt Education Ltd.

11 10 09 08 07
10 9 8 7 6 5 4 3 2 1

10 digit ISBN: 0 431 18309 0 (hardback)
13 digit ISBN: 978 0 431 18309 1
10 digit ISBN: 0 431 18316 3 (paperback)
13 digit ISBN: 978 0 431 18316 9

British Library Cataloguing in Publication Data

Parker, Steve
    Speed machines. - (The inside & out guides)
    1. Speed - Juvenile literature 2. Automobiles,
    racing - Juvenile literature 3. Motor vehicles
    - Juvenile literature
    I. Title
    629.2

Printed and bound in China

PHOTO CREDITS :

Abbreviations: t-top, m-middle, b-bottom, r-right,
l-left, c-centre.

6t, Nigel Kinrade Photography at autostockimages.com, 6b,
Peter Still at stillphotography.co.uk; 7, Nigel Kinrade
Photography at autostockimages.com; 8, McLaren; 9, Bugatti;
10, Eric Vargiolu; 11, Photo © Frédéric
Watbled/www.photographe-professionnel.fr; 12, Richard T
Bryant; 13, wikipedia.org; 14t, wikipedia.org, 14b, Bob Plumer
at 70sfunnycars.com; 15, Auto Imagery Inc; 16, wikipedia.org;
18t, Simon Bradley at motorbikestoday.com, 18b,
nexusracing.co.uk; 19, wikipedia.org; 20t, Fred Stevens at
warbird.com, 20b, Mike Massee/Xcor Aerospace; 21, Royal
Airforce Museum; 22, NASA; 23t, Steve Dean at Flight of the
Phoenix Aviation Museum, 23b, NASA; 24, NASA; 25t,m,b,
NASA; 26, Ken Warby; 27t, British Pathe/ITN; 28,
wikipedia.org; 29t,b, wikipedia.org

Every effort has been made to contact copyright
holders of any material reproduced in this book.
Any omissions will be rectified in subsequent
printings if notice is given to the publishers.

*An explanation of difficult words can be
found in the glossary on pages 30 and 31.*

The INSIDE & OUT *GUIDE to*
SPEED MACHINES

STEVE PARKER

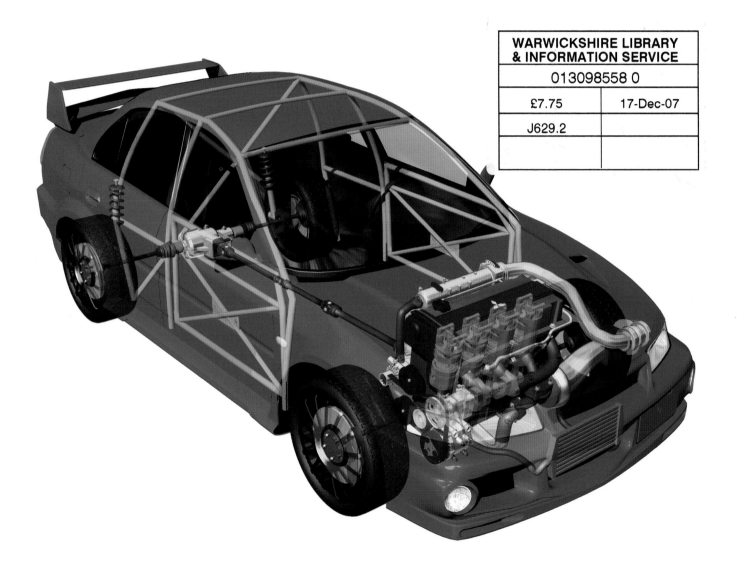

Heinemann
LIBRARY

CONTENTS

INTRODUCTION

SPEED BRINGS THRILLS – THE ROAR OF THE ENGINE, the surge of power, the wind on your face, and the scenery flashing past. On the road or rail, out at sea or in the sky, not much beats the excitement of a ride in a speed machine. This book opens up the insides of amazing craft and vehicles to reveal the cutting-edge technology beneath their super-streamlined shapes. It also shows how safety must always come first. Speed is a thrill – but it can also kill.

TOP STOCK CAR

The cars were originally 'stock', which means they came straight off the ordinary production line. Modern rules allow changes such as souped-up engines, plus of course, safety features such as the roll cage and specially shaped 'pilot' seat.

The United States' NASCAR (National Association for Stock Car Auto Racing) is the sport's biggest organization. It arranges 2,000 events yearly in twelve different divisions at over 100 oval race tracks. One of the great benefits, compared to Formula 1 or Rally Car racing, is that the crowds in the vast raceway stadium can see the whole event. Bumps and shoves are common. Serious crashes at over 250 km/h are rare but disastrous.

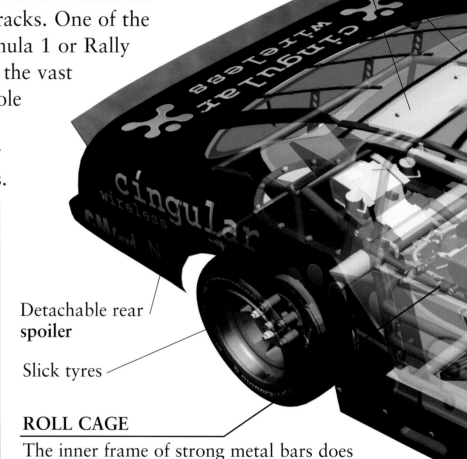

Roof flaps

Detachable rear **spoiler**

Slick tyres

ROLL CAGE

The inner frame of strong metal bars does not squash if the car crashes or rolls over. The shaped seat has padded wrap-around support, with harness belts around the shoulders and waist as well as between the legs.

BUILT TO BREAK

Crash technology means that most of the car bends, crumples, and absorbs the energy of a high-impact collision, keeping the driver safe.

BTCC

The British Touring Car Championships is the UK's top form of saloon car racing. About twelve teams battle it out over 30 rounds at nine or ten race circuits.

NASCAR CHEVROLET ROOF FLAPS, INTRODUCED IN 1994, RISE IF THE CAR SPINS TO PREVENT IT GETTING AIRBORNE AND FLIPPING OVER.

Driver Jeff 'Flash' Gordon started racing at five years old and signed to NASCAR in 1992. He has won the championship four times and has massive celebrity status, earning millions in advertising.

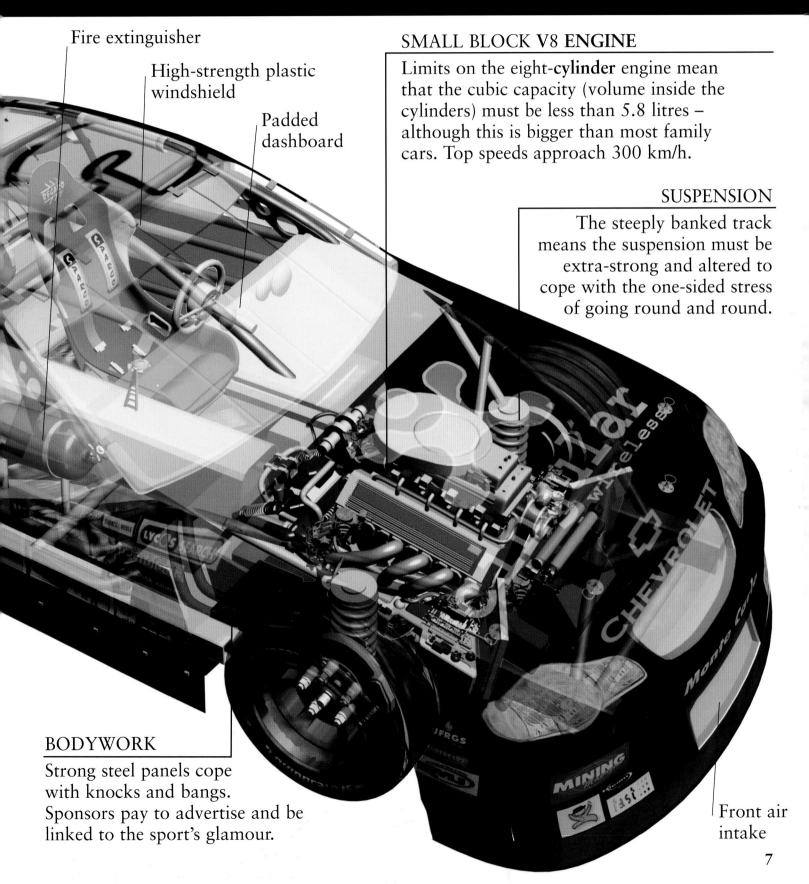

Fire extinguisher

High-strength plastic windshield

Padded dashboard

SMALL BLOCK V8 ENGINE

Limits on the eight-**cylinder** engine mean that the cubic capacity (volume inside the cylinders) must be less than 5.8 litres – although this is bigger than most family cars. Top speeds approach 300 km/h.

SUSPENSION

The steeply banked track means the suspension must be extra-strong and altered to cope with the one-sided stress of going round and round.

BODYWORK

Strong steel panels cope with knocks and bangs. Sponsors pay to advertise and be linked to the sport's glamour.

Front air intake

SPORTS SUPERCAR

FROM AN ADMIRING glance to a glare of pure envy, few speed machines attract such strong feelings as the sports supercar. You need no special training. Just buy one to drive – provided you're a millionaire.

Sports cars and roadsters are not particularly practical. They need open flat roads, regular maintenance, and careful tuning, with little space for the week's shopping. But they are a fabulous status symbol of the owner's wealth. The hand-built Bugatti Veyron is top of the tree, with a 16-cylinder engine rated at about 1,000 **horsepower** (**hp**) – more than a Formula 1 race car, and about six times as powerful as a typical family car. Its top speed of 407 km/h gave it the label of the world's fastest production car when it was introduced in 2005.

W16 ENGINE

Two V8 engines (the two banks of four cylinders are at an angle or 'V' to each other) are linked to form a W16. The engine is 8 litres in size yet weighs only 400 kilograms. Power is boosted by four **turbochargers**.

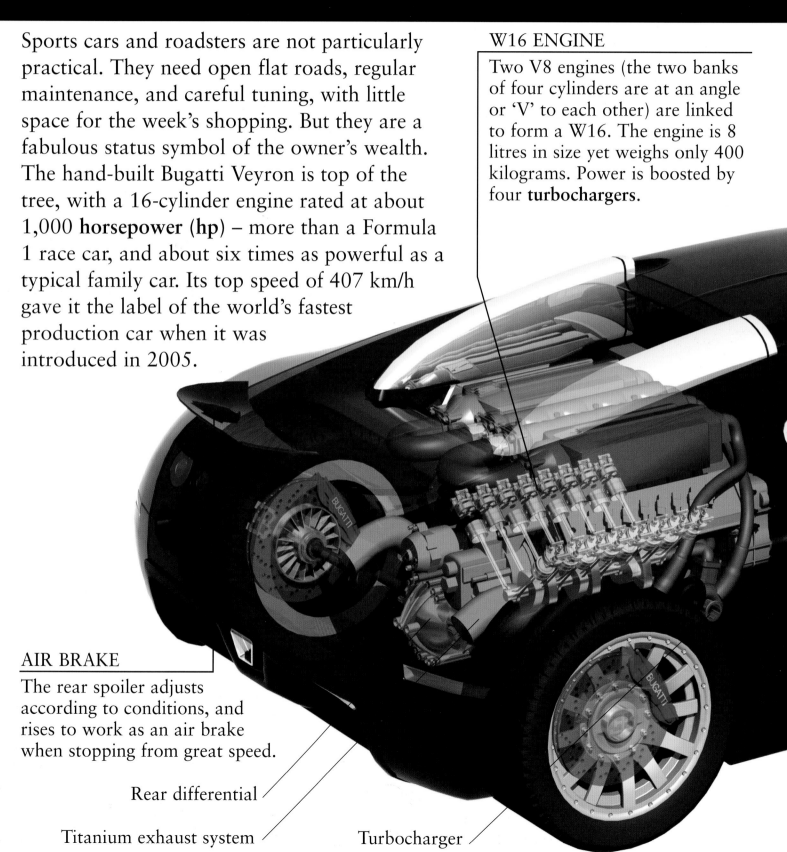

AIR BRAKE

The rear spoiler adjusts according to conditions, and rises to work as an air brake when stopping from great speed.

Rear differential

Titanium exhaust system

Turbocharger

BUGATTI VEYRON
THE BUGATTI VEYRON IS
THE WORLD'S FASTEST AND
MOST EXPENSIVE
PRODUCTION CAR, WITH A
PRICE TAG OF £685,000.

Ettore Bugatti (1881-1947) began
designing and making racing cars in
1909. His company has long made
distinctive vehicles. Its hand-made
Royale was the most expensive car
in the world at over £5,000,000.

DISC BRAKES

The brakes have huge ceramic discs and titanium **pistons**, with a design based partly on brakes in aircraft. They can slow the car from 100 km/h to standstill in just 31 metres.

FOUR WHEEL DRIVE

The seven-speed gearbox allows the world's fastest gear-shifting. The **torque** (turning power) to each wheel is automatically altered to prevent snaking or skidding by front and rear differentials.

CARBON FIBRE MONOCOQUE

The skin, or monocoque, of the car is carbon fibre, very light yet incredibly strong, stiff, and rustproof. In a crash it forms a 'survival cell' around the driver and passenger.

Alloy wheels

1990S SUPERCAR

In the 3-seat McLaren F1, the driver sat in the centre with two passengers behind. About 107 F1s were made in the 1990s. Until 2005, it was the fastest production road car at 386 km/h.

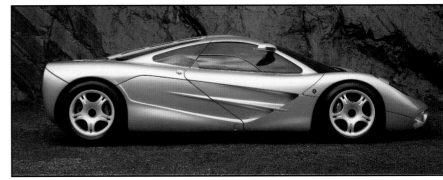

RALLY CAR CHAMP

RALLYING IS ONE OF the dirtiest and least comfortable motor sports. Cars slide along muddy tracks, bounce their drivers over rocks and pot holes, spray stones around corners, push through undergrowth, and splash through streams and puddles.

Rally drivers can pass through a whole year's motoring conditions in one day, from snow and ice to slippery leaf-strewn lanes to baking tarmac. Their cars are built for toughness and rugged reliability as well as speed. The co-driver in the passenger seat checks the route and warns the driver of upcoming bends and turns. A car can only be entered into the World Rally Championship if it is based on a type of production car that's made in quantities of more than 25,000 each year. Each of the 16 races of the Championship takes place in a different country.

Rear spoiler

ROLL CAGE

The driver and co-driver are protected inside a steel cage. The compartment is heavily padded to prevent injury on rough roads.

DESERT RACERS

The rally from Paris, France to Dakar, the capital of Senegal in West Africa, is truly gruelling. Much of the route is across the scorching Sahara Desert.

SUSPENSION

The heavily toughened suspension is based on the MacPherson strut design. In this the wheel's short 'stub axle' is at the end of a telescopic tilting arm. It's strong and easy to mend.

'DIFFS' AND FOUR-WHEEL DRIVE

Four-wheel drive transfers power through to all four wheels, through three differentials. The three 'diffs' allow wheels to move at different speeds when a vehicle is moving around a corner.

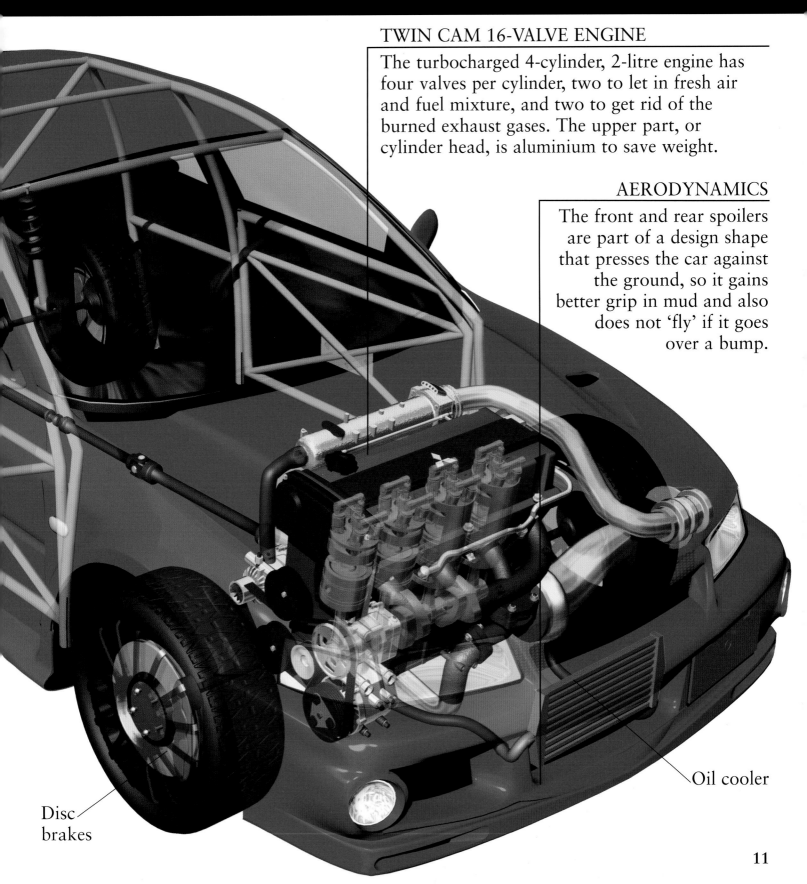

TWIN CAM 16-VALVE ENGINE

The turbocharged 4-cylinder, 2-litre engine has four valves per cylinder, two to let in fresh air and fuel mixture, and two to get rid of the burned exhaust gases. The upper part, or cylinder head, is aluminium to save weight.

AERODYNAMICS

The front and rear spoilers are part of a design shape that presses the car against the ground, so it gains better grip in mud and also does not 'fly' if it goes over a bump.

Oil cooler

Disc brakes

TOP RACER

FORMULA 1 IS THE ULTIMATE TEST OF DRIVER and car. No racing vehicle has such a combination of acceleration, top speed, braking power, handling agility, and cornering ability. These machines and their drivers are tested on tracks around the globe.

F1 IN NORTH AMERICA
Canada hosts a yearly F1 race, but in the United States 'Indy' (Indianapolis) oval-track races are more popular.

In the F1 (Formula One) World Championship, ten to twelve teams, each with two drivers, compete in 18 to 20 races. These are held one to two weeks apart across nearly every continent, from March to September. A massive 'circus' of cars, drivers, spares, mechanics, pit crew, managers, support staff, sponsors, and media – more than 10,000 people – fly from one twisting circuit to the next, almost taking over each host city. More than 200,000 spectators cram into the biggest tracks. Races are about 300 kilometres long.

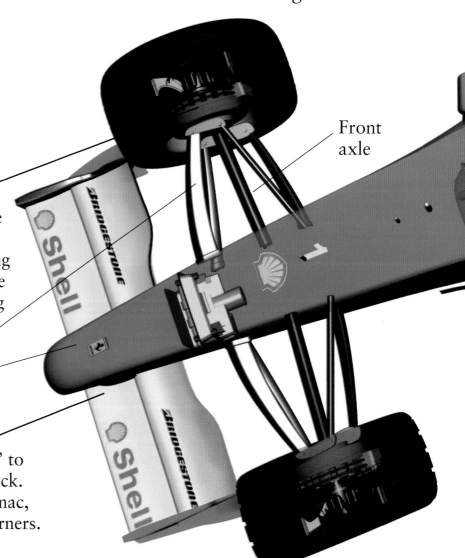

Front axle

BRAKES

Drivers brake hard at the last possible moment for every corner, putting incredible strain on the all-disc braking system. ABS or 'anti-lock' brakes were tried but banned in the 1990s to bring back drivers' skill.

Steering arm

Aerodynamic nose cone

FRONT SPOILER

The wing-like spoiler uses 'reverse lift' to press the front of the car on to the track. This keeps the tyres firmly on the tarmac, increasing the speed a car can turn corners.

FERRARI F1
A TYPICAL F1 CAR HAS
15,000 COMPONENTS, OR
PARTS. FOUR THOUSAND
OF THESE ARE FOUND IN
THE ENGINE.

German Michael Schumacher has dominated F1 Grand Prix ('Great Prize') races in recent years, with 84 race wins to 2005. He has won more races than any other driver in history.

BODY SHAPE

Every part of the car's surface is tested by computer modelling and in a wind tunnel. Various positions and shapes are even tried for the rear-view mirrors.

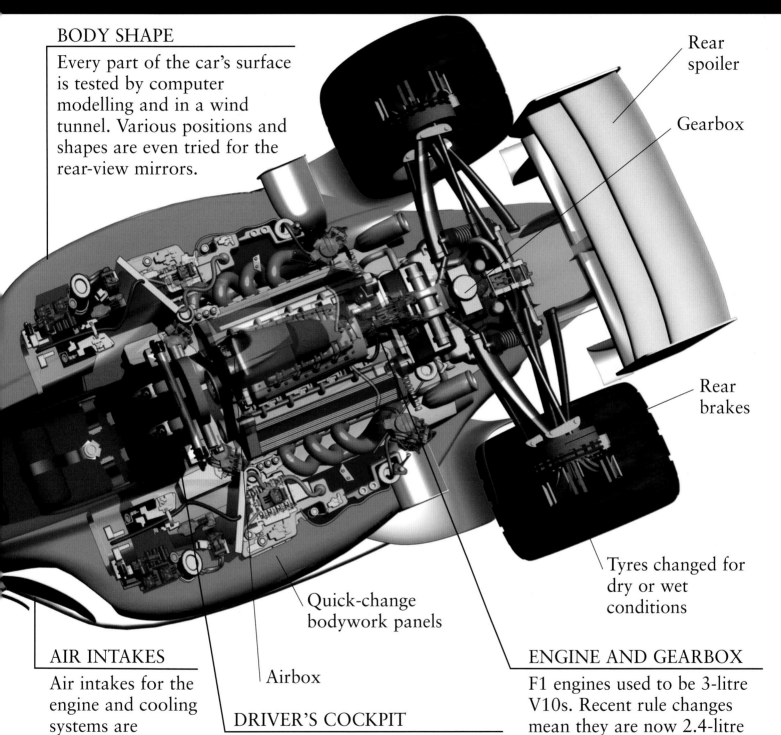

Rear spoiler

Gearbox

Rear brakes

Tyres changed for dry or wet conditions

Quick-change bodywork panels

Airbox

AIR INTAKES

Air intakes for the engine and cooling systems are positioned in the fronts of the side pods and in the airbox above the driver's helmet.

DRIVER'S COCKPIT

The reinforced cockpit keeps the driver safe in the event of a crash. He or she is able to communicate with the **pit team** while driving over a wireless connection.

ENGINE AND GEARBOX

F1 engines used to be 3-litre V10s. Recent rule changes mean they are now 2.4-litre V8s with a six- or seven-speed gearbox. These are less powerful – but reduced track speed means better safety.

DRAGSTER

A VERY specialized race car, the dragster does just one thing – it speeds as quickly as possible over a straight quarter-mile (402 metres).

Drag racing is tense, noisy, and spectacular, but the real action occurs in very short bursts. The top cars can cover the standard quarter-mile 'strip' from a standing start in less than five seconds. After just half a second of acceleration the speed is already 100 km/h. As the dragster roars over the finish line it is almost flying at up to 530 km/h. Usually there are two cars in each race. But all times are recorded to decide on the overall winner.

BURNOUT
Before starting, the rear tyres are covered with water and spun against the ground to improve their grip.

COCKPIT
The specially fitted, padded seat must cushion the driver against face-flattening forces of more than 5 g – five times the normal pull of gravity.

Fuel tank

GUIDE WHEELS
Thin wheels hold up the very light front end, and simple steering allows the driver to keep a straight line if the car 'slews' to the side.

FUNNY CARS
A funny car is a 'dragster in disguise' – a hugely powerful engine in front, and massive rear tyres, all inside the body shell of an ordinary production car.

TOP FUEL DRAGSTER
BURNING A MIXTURE OF
1/10TH METHANOL AND
9/10THS NITROMETHANE
YIELDS OVER TWICE THE
ENERGY OF PETROL.

Wally Parks (b. 1913) made his first 'hot rod' from an army jeep in World War Two. From the 1950s he took drag racing, and other forms of hot-rodding from dangerous, illegal road races to exciting, respectable sports.

SUPERCHARGED V8 ENGINE

Each of the eight cylinders may have a capacity ('size') larger than a small family car engine. Power output is a phenomenal 800-plus brake hp.

AEROFOIL

The aerofoil 'wing' helps to keep the rear end down and moving in a straight line.

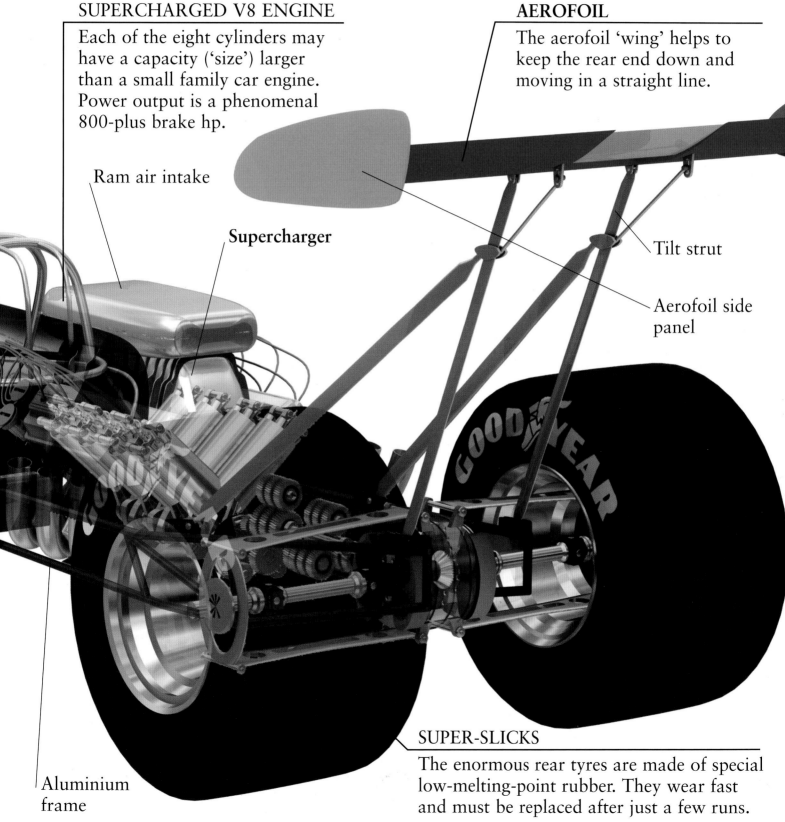

Ram air intake

Supercharger

Tilt strut

Aerofoil side panel

Aluminium frame

SUPER-SLICKS

The enormous rear tyres are made of special low-melting-point rubber. They wear fast and must be replaced after just a few runs.

RECORD BREAKER

The first official land speed record was set in France in 1898 by Gaston de Chasseloup-Laubat, driving a Jeantaud electric car at 63 km/h. Green's record-breaking run 99 years later was almost 20 times faster, at almost 1,230 km/h. 'SSC' means '**SuperSonic** Car' – faster than sound. *Thrust SSC*'s two-way run was timed at Mach 1.02, that is, 1.02 times the speed of sound. BOOM!

Rear wheel

Frame chassis

Afterburner

PARACHUTE BRAKES

One 2.2-metre parachute slowed the car to below 1,000 km/h, then three more parachutes took it down to 650 km/h, when carbon disc brakes on the wheels were deployed.

BLUE FLAME
In 1970, Gary Gabelich was first to exceed the 1,000 km/h mark in Blue Flame, *with a speed of 1,001.66 km/h.*

JET TURBINE POWER

A large fan-like turbine sucked air into the engine's combustion chamber. When the fuel had been burned away, the afterburner sprayed in extra fuel for the air to burn, which created even more exhaust to power the machine.

THRUST SSC
ALMOST 15 METRES LONG
AND 3.35 METRES WIDE
THRUST SSC WEIGHED
NEARLY 10 TONNES, PLUS
ONE TONNE OF JET FUEL.

RAF Squadron Leader Andy
Green (right) took Thrust SSC's
controls. The previous record-
holder in Thrust 2, Richard
Noble, was Thrust's project
director and chief fundraiser.

SONIC BOOM

Shock waves of air piled up in front of Thrust SSC and were compressed into a wall of sound, causing a giant thunderclap of a sonic boom.

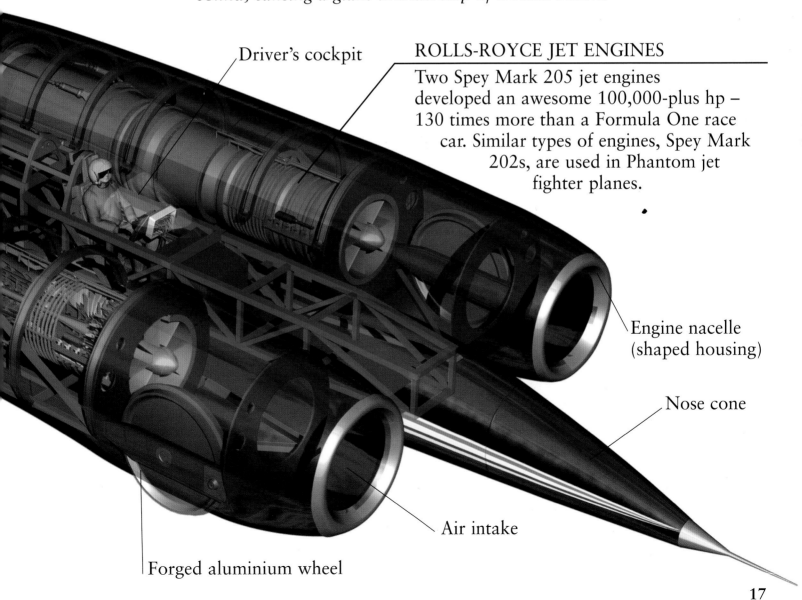

Driver's cockpit

ROLLS-ROYCE JET ENGINES

Two Spey Mark 205 jet engines developed an awesome 100,000-plus hp – 130 times more than a Formula One race car. Similar types of engines, Spey Mark 202s, are used in Phantom jet fighter planes.

Engine nacelle
(shaped housing)

Nose cone

Air intake

Forged aluminium wheel

RACING BIKE

gears, the Superbike leans into the corner at an almost impossible angle, whips around the curve, and with an ear-splitting engine whine, zooms away in a haze of exhaust and dust. In three seconds it's gone.

Motorcycle World Championships have different classes for engine sizes from 80 cc (0.08 litres) through 125 and 250 to 500 cc. These thoroughbred racing machines need total control by skilled riders making life-or-death decisions every split-second. The Superbike class can have larger engines, up to 1,000 cc, with two, three or four cylinders. They are modified versions of road bikes and so are less rapid than pure race bikes – but are still spectacular to watch.

ROUND THE BEND
Motorcyclists wear strong protective suits called 'leathers' in case they slip or skid, with thickened knee pads to graze the tarmac around corners.

Aluminium beam chassis frame

Stainless steel exhaust system

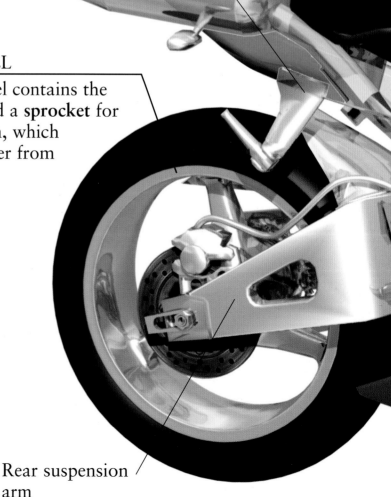

REAR WHEEL
The rear wheel contains the disc brake and a **sprocket** for the final chain, which transfers power from the engine.

TWO'S COMPANY
In sidecars at bends, the co-rider stretches far to the left or leans over behind the rider.

Rear suspension arm

HONDA CBR600RR THE LATEST TECHNOLOGY OF THE MOTOGP RACE BIKE WAS IMMEDIATELY USED IN THE CBR600RR ROAD VERSION.

Italian ace Valentino Rossi is the most successful motorcycle racer of all time. From 1997 to 2005, he won seven World Grand Prix titles with bikes by Aprilia, Honda, and Yamaha.

HIGH PERFORMANCE ENGINE

Most Superbike engines produce 180–200 hp at 13,000–14,000 rpm (revolutions per minute). Maximum speed is generally over 300 km/h and average lap speeds are between 170 and 200 km/h depending on the circuit.

DISC BRAKES

The huge discs have different composite alloys for the inner and outer portions, with ventilation slots and holes to help cooling.

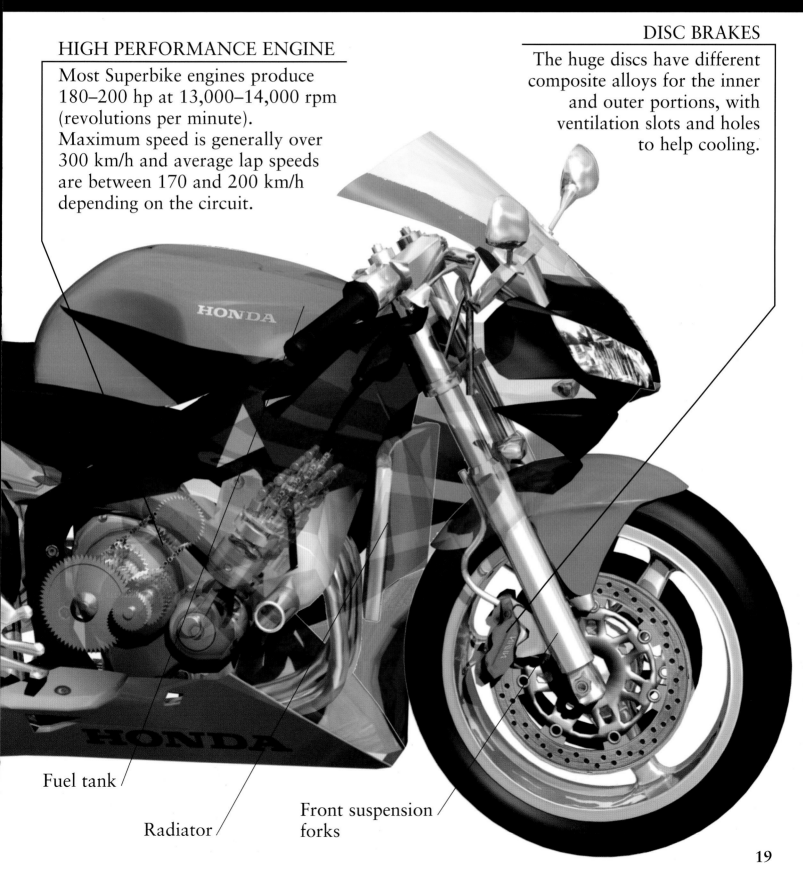

Fuel tank

Radiator

Front suspension forks

AIR RACER

CARS RACE. SO DO TRUCKS, HOVERCRAFT, submarines – and planes. The fastest aircraft zoom round lap after lap in a battle of speed, manoeuvrability, and bravery.

CLASSIC RACERS

T-6 class racers are based on the legendary World War Two fighter-training plane known variously as the T-6 Texan, SNJ, or Harvard.

Propeller-driven classes of aero racers include biplanes, kit-build aircraft, 'stock' planes slightly modified from the manufacturer, and super-sportsters like the Gee Bees (named after their makers, the four Granville Brothers from Springfield, Massachusetts). Races started after World War One (1914–1918) as pilots thrilled air show crowds with speed and aerobatics. It's not just raw power in aero racing that makes it exciting. The huge-engined, small-airframe craft are tricky to fly and pilots use air currents and opponent's slipstreams in their race strategies.

Tail **fin**

Landing skid

ROCKET RACER

The Rocket Racing League, which began in 2005, features modified craft based on the EZ-Rocket 'X-plane'. The X-racers can go at 350 km/h but only for four minutes!

WING

The wings were specially strengthened against enormous forces in tight turns. The two long spars bore about 20 ribs that ran between the leading and trailing edges.

Aileron

GEE BEE MODEL Z
THE MODEL Z HAD A
7.2-METRE WINGSPAN,
WAS 4.6 METRES LONG,
AND WEIGHED 1,214 KG
WHEN FULLY LOADED.

The Gee Bee R-1 first flew in August 1932. Pilot Jimmy Doolittle won that year's Thompson Trophy with an average speed of 407 km/h.

COCKPIT
The pilot sat almost under the front of the very low tail fin, to balance the large engine at the front.

Engine cowling, or covering

Wing upper tensioning wire

PROPELLER
The twin-bladed propeller supplied all the force needed to pull the plane through the air at a top speed of 470 km/h.

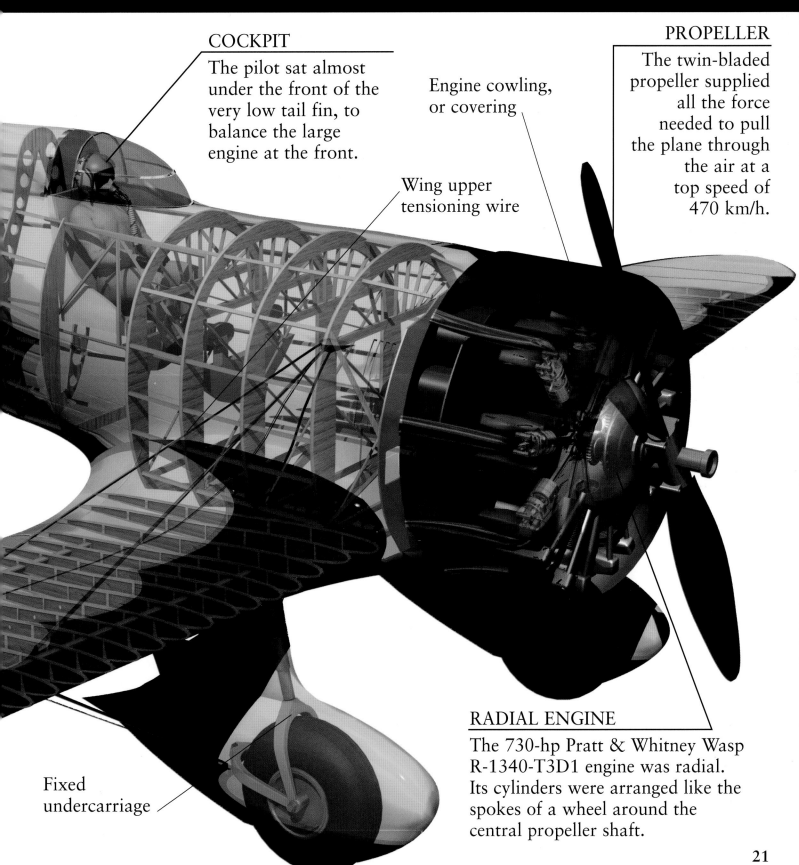

Fixed undercarriage

RADIAL ENGINE
The 730-hp Pratt & Whitney Wasp R-1340-T3D1 engine was radial. Its cylinders were arranged like the spokes of a wheel around the central propeller shaft.

BLACKBIRD

Lockheed SR-71 Blackbird as the most beautifully powerful machine ever built. Its air speed record for a non-rocket plane is over three times the speed of sound.

The US Air Force's Blackbird programme began in 1964 with plans for the fastest, highest-flying 'spy plane' ever built. The first SR-71 flew in December 1964. It was officially a 'strategic reconnaissance' aircraft. Because it flew so high, out of range of most radar systems and other planes, it went where it wanted to scan the scene with its own high-power radar system and take telescopic photographs. But as the rest of the world moved on, satellites took over spying duties. The SR-71's final mission was in 1997.

LONG LANDING
The SR-71 landed at 290 km/h and used a landing parachute to brake.

FUSELAGE FUEL TANK

At low speed the fuel tanks leaked – on purpose. As the plane went faster, and got hotter due to air **friction**, the metal tank panels expanded and closed gaps between them.

In-flight computer

Pressure suit

COCKPIT

The pilot sat in the front seat. The reconnaissance operator behind worked the radar, navigation, and photographic equipment.

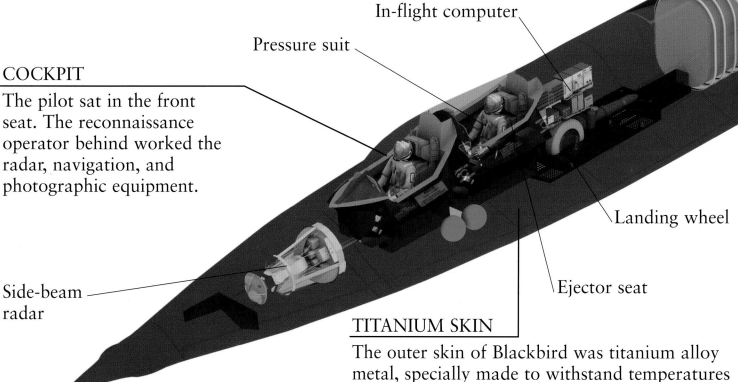

Landing wheel

Ejector seat

Side-beam radar

TITANIUM SKIN

The outer skin of Blackbird was titanium alloy metal, specially made to withstand temperatures of up to 1,000°C. The blue-black paint contained tiny radar-confusing iron spheres.

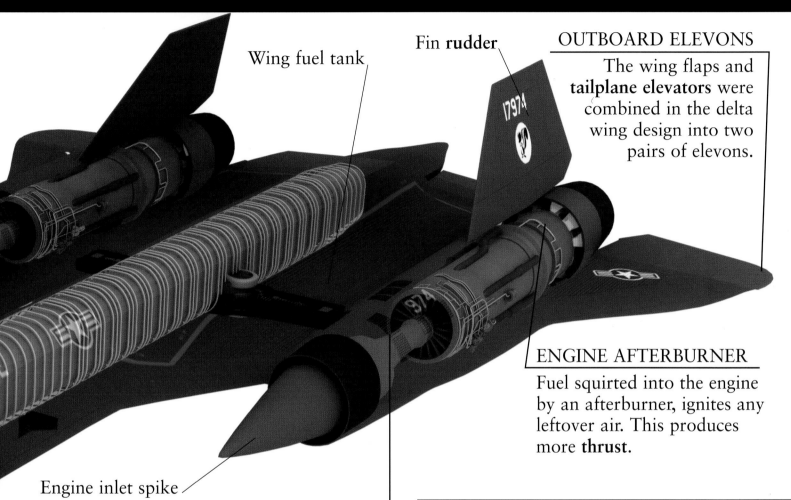

Wing fuel tank

Fin **rudder**

OUTBOARD ELEVONS

The wing flaps and **tailplane elevators** were combined in the delta wing design into two pairs of elevons.

ENGINE AFTERBURNER

Fuel squirted into the engine by an afterburner, ignites any leftover air. This produces more **thrust**.

Engine inlet spike

J58 JET ENGINE

Two Pratt & Whitney J58 jet engines produced 14,750 kg of thrust (160,000 hp). With a total fuel load of 45,000 litres, Blackbird had a maximum take-off weight of 77 tonnes and a range of almost 5,000 kms with its own fuel. This could be extended by mid-air refuelling.

SPY IN THE SKY

The USA used Blackbirds to keep an eye on foreign powers, especially the USSR, during the tense times between 1960 and 1970.

ROCKET PLANE

LONG BEFORE 'X-MEN' THERE were X-Planes, built by the USA to test aero-technology to the limit. Fastest and highest of all, with a rocket engine but still a plane rather than a true rocket, was the X-15.

Apart from spacecraft, the X-15 holds the record as the fastest speed machine on Earth – or rather, just above. Up to about 40 kilometres above the ground level, it flew as a real plane with wings and tail fins. However, as it approached space, (over 100 kilometres above the ground), small thruster rockets helped with flight control. Three X-15s were built, flying 199 research missions from 1959 to 1968.

BELL X-1
First X-plane, and first craft to go supersonic (faster than sound), was the Bell X-1. In October 1947 Charles 'Chuck' Yeager blasted through the sound barrier to 1,078 km/h.

FUEL TANK
The rocket engine burned a fuel called anhydrous ammonia, stored in extremely cold liquid form in the rear tank.

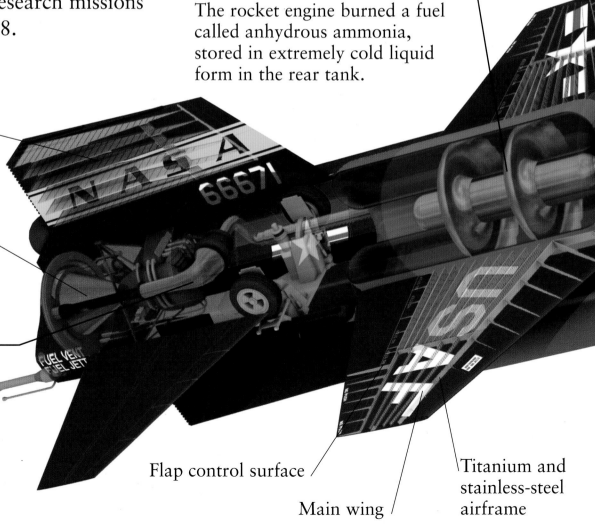

Tail fin

Rocket exhaust

XLR-99 ROCKET ENGINE
Replacing the XLR-11 on early X-15 trials, the XLR–99 produced 26,000 kg of thrust. It burned for 80 to 125 seconds depending on the mission.

Flap control surface

Main wing

Titanium and stainless-steel airframe

NORTH AMERICAN X-15
THE ONLY SPACECRAFT
THAT HAVE FLOWN HIGHER
THAN THE X-15 ARE THE
SPACE SHUTTLE AND
SPACESHIPONE.

Milt Thompson was one of only twelve X-15 pilots. Because several X-15 trips grazed the edge of space, six of the twelve pilots were given astronaut 'wings'.

OXYGEN TANK

Burning needs oxygen, and since there is almost none very high up, the X-15 took its own supply as ultra-cold liquid oxygen in the front tank.

MID-AIR LAUNCH

To save fuel the X-15 was slung under the wing of a massive 8-engined B-52 Stratofortress bomber and taken up to about 10,000 metres before release.

Nickel-chromium outer skin

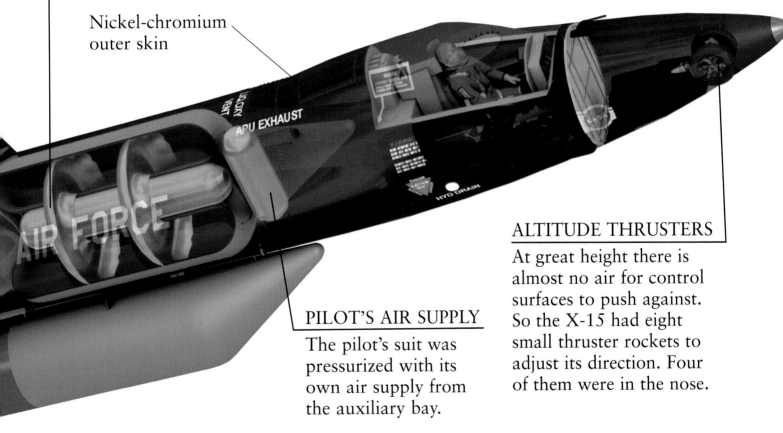

ALTITUDE THRUSTERS

At great height there is almost no air for control surfaces to push against. So the X-15 had eight small thruster rockets to adjust its direction. Four of them were in the nose.

PILOT'S AIR SUPPLY

The pilot's suit was pressurized with its own air supply from the auxiliary bay.

SAFE TOUCHDOWN

The X-15 was 16 metres long, with a wingspan of 6.7 metres. After the rocket burn it became a superfast glider for ten minutes, then landed at 320 km/h.

POWERBOAT

IF YOU LIKE DEAFENING NOISE AND bone-shaking bashes at breakneck speed, powerboat racing is for you. It's one of the toughest fast-action sports as boats going twice the motorway speed limit slam into waves up to 2 metres high – WHAM!

Apart from speed, toughness and safety are powerboat racing's key words. What seems like a small surface ripple can knock you out of your seat when hit at more than 250 kilometres per hour. Drivers and crew are firmly strapped into specially-shaped, extra-padded seats. Some powerboats are single-hulled, while others are designed as a catamaran, with two narrow hulls joined by a central platform. Air trapped between the two hulls lifts the boat as it picks up speed. This gives it less drag in the water so it can skim across the surface.

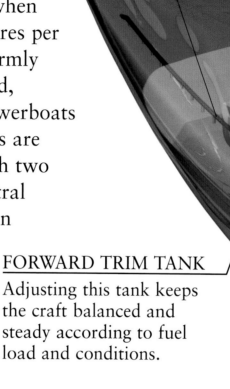

Spray rail

Aluminium hull

FORWARD TRIM TANK
Adjusting this tank keeps the craft balanced and steady according to fuel load and conditions.

FUEL TANKS
The hull holds two enormous fuel tanks. During a race, the gas-guzzling engines can use about 180 litres of fuel an hour. The fuel is pumped from two tanks to ensure that the boat stays even.

UNBROKEN RECORD
The water speed record was set in 1978 when Ken Warby piloted the hydroplane Spirit of Australia *to 511 km/h on Blowering Dam Lake, New South Wales, Australia.*

Son of record-breaker Malcolm Campbell, Donald Campbell died tragically in 1967. He was attempting to break a water speed record in Bluebird K7, on Coniston Water in England.

V12 ENGINES

Typically the 8.2-litre engines come from sports car makers, especially Lamborghini. They have an inboard position, within the main hull, rather than outboard (see right).

Throttle lever

OUTBOARDS

Some powerboats have engines outside the hull, known as outboards, giving more room for repair. The whole engine swivels to steer.

Rear trim tank

SUPERFAST PROPELLER

The small-bladed propeller (prop) spins 150 times each second, on a long shaft to stay in the water. A particular prop from a choice of ten or more is selected according to the race conditions.

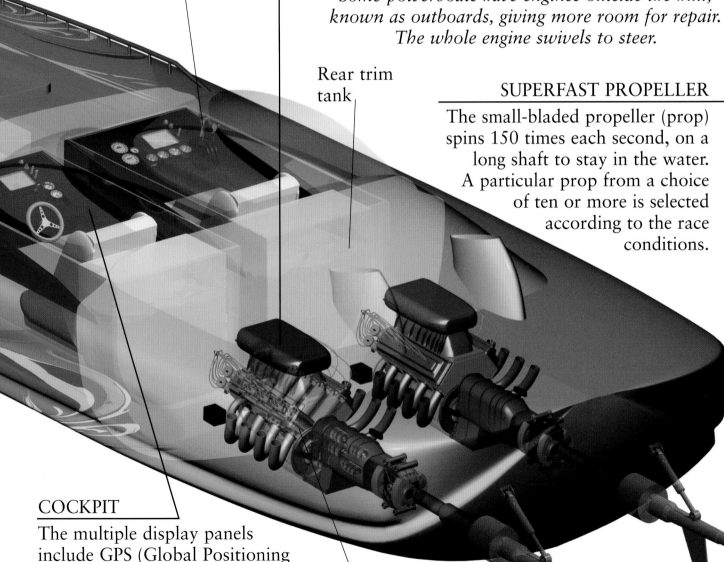

COCKPIT

The multiple display panels include GPS (Global Positioning System), engine read-outs, trim indicators, and warning lights.

Engine exhausts

HIGH SPEED TRAIN

ZOOM, SWISH, WHIZZ – the bullet train goes so fast you cannot notice stations or small villages. You pass through a large town in just a few seconds.

Bullet trains began in 1964 in Japan, where they are called *shinkansen*. The idea was to travel at great speed, comfortably, and reliably, without cars choking roads. Bullet-type trains spread to France with the TGV or *Train à Grande Vitesse* (very fast train), also the TAVs in Italy, Spain's AVEs, Germany's ICEs, Korea's KTXs and Britain's InterCity 125 (125 mph or 200 km/h). The world rail speed record is held by a TGV specially modified for high-speed research, which raced along a brand new track near Tours, in France, at 515.3 kilometres per hour in May 1990.

MAGLEV
Magnetic levitation trains 'float' above the track by magnetic forces. China's Shanghai airport-city link tops 430 km/h.

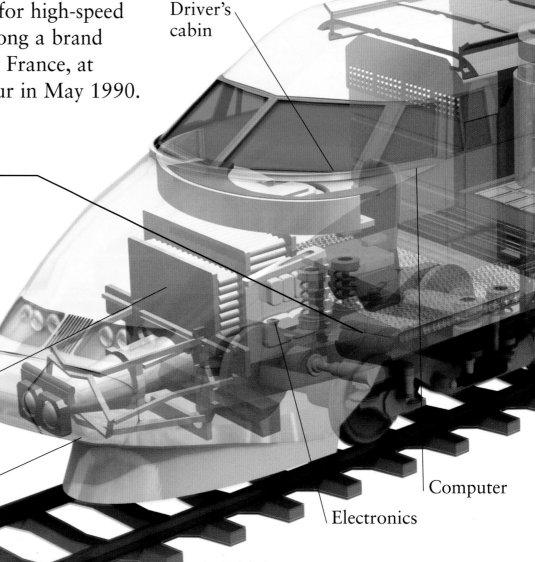

Driver's cabin

ELECTRIC MOTORS

The front three bogies (frames with wheels that support the carriage) have electric motors to power the wheels.

Impact block

Automatic coupling

Electronics

Computer

TGV High Speed Train
The *TGV Atlantique*, designed for the coast route by the Atlantic Ocean, usually travels at 300 km/h.

Inside high speed trains, such as the shinkansen *bullet train, passengers relax in great comfort. On some lines the whole train tilts so people are not flung sideways going around sharper corners.*

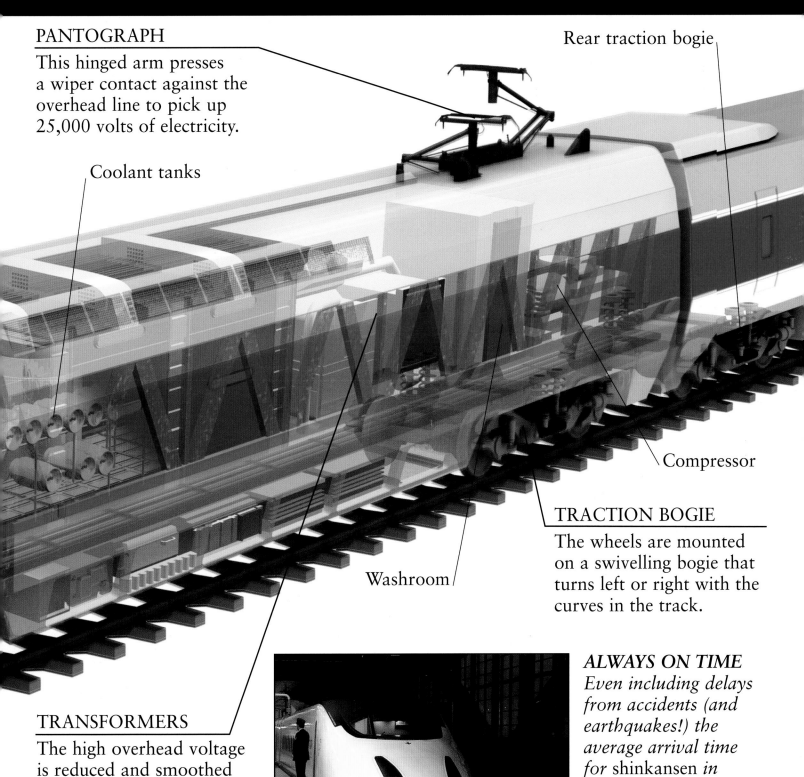

PANTOGRAPH
This hinged arm presses a wiper contact against the overhead line to pick up 25,000 volts of electricity.

Coolant tanks

Rear traction bogie

Compressor

TRACTION BOGIE
The wheels are mounted on a swivelling bogie that turns left or right with the curves in the track.

Washroom

TRANSFORMERS
The high overhead voltage is reduced and smoothed out for the motors by massive, well-cooled transformers.

ALWAYS ON TIME
Even including delays from accidents (and earthquakes!) the average arrival time for shinkansen *in 2003 was within 6 seconds of its scheduled times.*

GLOSSARY

acceleration
The gaining of speed.

aerofoil
A wing that produces an upwards force, to lift an aeroplane, or a downwards force, as in racing cars.

afterburner
A device that burns leftover air in the exhaust gases from a jet engine, to give extra thrust (pushing power).

aileron
Flap-like surfaces usually along the rear of an aeroplane's main wings, which tilt to make the plane bank (lean) to the left or right.

carbon fibre
A very strong, light material made of tiny strands or fibres of carbon. It can be more than twice as stiff as steel.

cylinder
In an engine, a chamber that houses the piston, which moves up and down inside it.

disc brake
A brake design in which stationary brake pads press against a ring-like disc attached to the road wheel.

elevators
Flap-like surfaces usually along the rear of an aeroplane's tailplane, which tilt to make the plane go up or down.

fin
The upright flat surface or 'tail' usually at the rear end of an aeroplane, to which the rudder is attached.

friction
The resistance caused by two surfaces rubbing against each other. It always creates heat.

horsepower (hp)
A measure of power, widely used for engines and vehicles of all kinds.

hot rod
A wheeled vehicle that has been modified and improved to be much more powerful and go faster (and often look faster and better too).

piston
A solid metal cylinder that moves to and fro inside another, hollow cylinder.

pit team
A group of mechanics and engineers who work in the place where racing vehicles and speed machines are refuelled, adjusted, and repaired.

roll cage
Bars or struts that form a safety casing around a person, to protect him or her in case a vehicle rolls – turns on to its side and roof.

rudder
Flap-like surface usually on the rear of an aeroplane's fin, which swings to make the plane turn left or right.

spoiler
An aerofoil that affects the air flowing over it to create a downwards force, for example, by pressing a racing car down on to the track for better grip.

sprocket
A wheel with a set of teeth around its rim.

stock
Standard or unmodified version, of a car, plane, or machine, as bought from the manufacturer's 'stock'.

supercharger
A device in an engine, driven by a belt, chain, or gears from the main engine shaft, that pushes air at high pressure into the cylinders to increase power.

supersonic
Faster than the speed of sound, which is not a standard measurement as it varies with the material through which it travels. In air, it is 1,200km/h.

tailplane
Small horizontal rear wings usually at the rear of an aeroplane, which generally carry the elevators.

thrust
A strong continuous force.

torque
Turning force, for example, the amount of turning force produced by an engine.

turbocharger
An engine supercharger that is driven by a fan-like turbine, spun by exhaust gases, to increase engine power.

USSR
A group of countries, including Russia, that broke up in 1991.

V engine (such as V8, V10)
An engine with two banks of cylinders at an angle to each other, to form a 'V'.

INDEX